The Lost Snacks

by Holly Harper
illustrated by Sofia Cardoso

OXFORD
UNIVERSITY PRESS

Greta and Clint were camping with Grandma. They picked a spot on the embankment.

They set up the tent.

“Twist in the peg,” said Grandma.

Greta squinted at the brush. "Did you hear that?"

"It was me," moaned Clint.
"I'm starving!"

"Get a sandwich from the lunchbox," said Grandma.

"Come and help with the trunk,"
said Grandma.

Greta left her sandwich on the log.

Greta was shocked. “Just the crust is left! Clint is tricking me!” she said.

"Do not fight," said Grandma.
"We have lots of snacks."

“It is so crisp!” said Greta.

Clint wished to keep his snack.
He put it on the trunk.

"No need to be a grump. You can have some of this," said Grandma.

Grandma got a shock. “That possum took the lost snacks!”

"He is so plump! I do not think the snacks are good for him," said Grandma.

Greta and Clint felt sad.

“We can get him some good food,” said Greta.

Greta got a gum tree branch. Clint picked a clump of green fronds.

Grandma laid out a blanket. They all sat down for dinner.

Look Back

Encourage students to use the pictures to retell the story.